WAITING FOR
Red

K.L. Schoberg

Orange Hat Publishing
www.orangehatpublishing.com - Waukesha, WI

For information, please contact:

Orange Hat Publishing
www.orangehatpublishing.com
Waukesha, WI

Photography by Anthony Larson
Cover typography by Kelly Maddern

for those who crave the color Red
but lay in fields of white instead

VOLUME 1

VOLUME 2

VOLUME 1

THE PORTAL

What is it you
are waiting for?
Wonder lurks
'hind wooden doors!

Darkness rains like
vulture's wings;
be prepared
for peculiar things.

Though I cannot
tell you why,
snow falls upwards
towards the sky.

Close the door
so very tight!
'Tis not a place
for evening light.

Beware, beware
as you embark;
rhymes run rabid
in the dark.

Please don't wander
far ahead!
I've been waiting, waiting, waiting
for Red.

SCARLET KNIGHT

On an autumn, autumn night
She was born with auburn hair
She mirrored her mother's loving stare
Quickly wrapped in sheets of white
They named her Scarlet Knight.

Scarlet, Scarlet Knight
Turned the blooming age of two
She danced, she danced in ruby shoes
Her mother watched in pure delight
Scarlet blew out her birthday lights.

Scarlet, Scarlet Knight
Indulged the age of twenty-two
Drank the wine as lovers do
Since her first sip was not right
Scarlet wore her cloak of white.

On an autumn, autumn night
Scarlet turned the age of forty-five
She dreamed, she beamed, she was alive
Beautiful, kind, she spoke polite
Scarlet bathed in blissful light.

On an autumn, autumn night
She sang into the evening hues
She slipped off her mother's dancing shoes
Scarlet held her mother tight
And wrapped her in a sheet of white.

FIELDS OF COTTON

Have I simply just forgotten
Why I trundle fields of cotton?
Seems every time I search for red,
I find myself in white instead.

Like when I hunt for amelia rose,
Sunlight warms my summer toes.
As I roam through open pasture,
I pick only petals of white aster.

Why do I wander orchard hills
With a basket only I can fill?
When I pick a fruit to take a bite,
All the bitter apples are white.

I ought not travel in this fashion,
For red is love, and red is passion!
I only see the whitest winds.
Perhaps this is how my story begins.

THE POEM

Poetry is the tiny portal
where darkness and light unite.
It's the redemption of morning,
the tender forgiveness of night.

Poetry is fireflies in winter,
snowflakes in July.
It's a hologram of love
who passed us by.

Poetry is the sky when
storm clouds dance.
It's the cleansing sigh
of a second chance.

Poetry is north, south,
west and east.
It's slithering steam
off sun-drenched streets.

Poetry is a revolting shadow,
silk dress and smoking gun.
It's the unexpected ending
and how the story begun.

SAKURA

I softly breathe beneath
a wind-kissed tree
petals swarm
a fleeting dream

A union of red
and wondrous white
storm of desire
delights of night

We will meet beneath
a wind-kissed tree
cherry petal songs
of lost serenity

I long to wake
beside his breath
minutes march betwixt
my birth, my death

I softly breathe beneath
a wind-kissed tree
petals swarm
a fleeting dream

ROSE CANDY TEA

Wonder where I'm going? I'll give you a hint.
Apricot, coconut, lemongrass mint!

Irish rose, orange spice, shall I repeat?
I'm headed to the shop at the end of the street.

Ring, ring, ding-a-ling, samba inside,
So many sweet teas, I can't decide.

Chai tea, Thai tea, golden monkey,
Sangria, I'll meet ya for white peony tea.

One dollar, two dollars, next comes three,
The little tea shop sells rose candy tea!

WHO SLEEPS AMONGST THE REDWOODS?

There is a place, and unusual space,
Countless moons away
Where towering trees have eyes
And feet are wedged in clay.

Who sleeps amongst the redwoods
When nightfall shrouds the sun?
An owl, a flower sleep only an hour
When the dwindling day is done.

Trees rustle, snap, rumble, and rap
As the sky hails vulture wings.
I wouldn't dare find myself there
If the withering winds should sing.

Sleep, sleep the redwood trees
Rest triumphs to only some
Sway, pray for one more day
The daybreak rays will come.

WOLF IN A SHEEP'S NEGLIGEE

In a dark, dark dream
she couldn't escape
strolled a woman
in a crimson cape.

Over the bridge,
through starless streets,
she embarked on a quest
only she could complete.

Though she carried
her basket of bread,
the coat of a wolf
would never be shed.

She rapped upon
yesterday's door
with big green eyes
he couldn't ignore.

Little Miss shot
a sheepish grin, then
howled out loud,
"I've done it again."

Passion, passion
was she seduced?
The wolf, the wolf
the wolf was on the loose.

LOVE SONG OF DRAGON MOUNTAIN

Soar with me
    'pon dragon wings,
        through humble winds we'll fly.
            Embers fade from sunset
                replaced by blackened sky.

Embrace me tightly
    in this world bereft of words.
        Hear the melody, the love song
            of the cape sugar birds.

Rise and fall like hope;
    skies are wavy as sea!
        Dragon Mountain
            softly whispers,
                Whatever will be, will be.

NOWHERE STREET

Someone lives on the end of Nowhere Street
The most beautiful kind I'll never meet.

He wrapped his yard with broken gate
Did I arrive two steps too late?

Knock, knock, knock on Someone's door
He does, he lives here! That I'm sure.

Greeted by the strangest frown,
"Your someone, he lives three doors down!"

Three doors down, on Nowhere Street
Lives the kindest man I'll never meet.

Though I waited and waited and turned around
Someone knocked first, just three doors down.

BUTTERFLY WHISPERS

Tiny wings flutter
Weeks ago
My conscience buzzes

Sun-kissed field
Stretched for miles
Time flitters by

Tiny whispers
Butterfly voices
Not premonitions
But guidance

I hear them now
Yesterday's butterflies

Reminding me to turn around
Leave the windy path
Backwards, barefoot

I return to the
Sun-kissed field
Stretched for miles

I listen closely
As butterflies whisper
I wonder if the whispers today
Will be heard in weeks to come?

Soft sounds of regret
Whispers turn to screams

STONY HOLLOW ROAD

A figure lurks upon a cliff
on Stony Hollow Road,
a woman awaits a perilous fate,
a grim folklore unfolds.

Her lover was out quite late
that fated autumn night;
did he gently clasp another
under callous candlelight?

Lucinda, Lucinda, Lucinda,
a crying crow in pain,
dove to Stony Hollow Road,
a destined romance slain.

Many a moonrise later,
three whispers chant her name;
she knows not why they mock her,
their demise will be the same!

A screeching crow flies north
'bove thrashing poplar trees;
night exhales red-mist breath,
a slapping bone-cold breeze.

PAPER LANTERN

Mild aroma of
    wild orchids
a ceremony begins
       red lantern
    gently hovers
like a ghost
    to spirit winds
       A greying sky
          begins to mist
             entanglements
       now free
     clouds drop tears upon tears
    as I release you
to sea

The winds remember
    as you climb toward
       horizon's last
          ember.

HAIKU FOR THE ROBINS

Unquiet sky wails
Red feathers rumba westward
Dance, dance the robins

BURNING CITY

Once upon
    a burning city
        softly sleeping
    close of day

        Smoke slithered
        a withered path

                through midnight
                alleyways

ashes, ravens, rage, dust
embers, fire, fury, lust!

                buildings crumble,
                one by one

        can this wreckage
        be undone?

peace, promise, trust, love
snowfall, glory, grace, a dove

                once upon a faithful city
                gently lifting,
                      break of day,
                concrete roses rise and pray

TEN BALLOONS

I once held ten balloons
I aimed them at the first full moon

One was for hatred
Two for hurt
Three for the stain on my favorite shirt
Four for miserable mistakes
Five for burdens I couldn't take
Six for anger boiled and built
Seven for my enemy, guilt
Eight for everything I lack
Nine is where I lost track

Then at the breaking dawn of day
I thought the balloons all floated away
I reached out my hand and closed my eyes
Down from the clouds came a surprise

The last one was for kindness, you see
It was the only one that was meant for me

THE POSTMAN

Darkness thieved the night of blue
In the air, a malevolent chill
On the hour the owl stood guard
A haunting rolled over the hill.

He gripped a satchel of letters
Leather hat obscured his thought
A single whip on the horse's hip
No one knew the postman's plot.

The moon a soundless witness
To a carriage upon cobblestones
Rocking to the whining of wind
As cold as forgotten bones.

He reached inside his satchel
Pulled out the one in red
Let the cold wind snatch it
Like a falcon, it quickly fled.

The carriage halted on command
He rapped upon her door
A woman in white waited all night
For a letter she was longing for.

He dug inside his satchel
Then simply shook his head
Like whispering wind, she sighed
It wasn't her time for Red.

Darkness thieved the night of blue
In the air, a malevolent chill
On the hour the owl stood guard
A haunting rolled over the hill.

BALLAD OF THE BANYAN

What lies beneath the banyan tree
If roots grow above the ground?
One moonlit night I dug and dug
Befuddled by what I found.

I stuck my head below to peek
Though did not expect to see
Birds swarming the underworld
Whirling 'pon mirrored tree.

Glowing branches swayed;
Could this be purely chance?
Whenever wind blew from above,
Below the cardinals danced.

Have you ever cared to wonder
What lies beneath the banyan tree?
I found, I found, I found it!
A backwards world we cannot see.

VOLUME 2

BLOOD WOLF MOON

Snow gusts and creaky howl,
A single wolf begins her prowl.
Wind rambles a wicked tune:
Blood. Wolf. Moon.

Earth will shadow 'pon the sky,
Red ravens will no longer fly.
Fiery hues ignite the night!
Blood. Wolf. Moon.

Some say the sun shall fade,
Pillars of smoke will rise, invade,
Black will awake and overtake.
Blood. Wolf. Moon.

Moon passes in front of sun,
A lone wolf, I am just one.
The eclipse will stir apocalypse!
Blood. Wolf. Moon.

JUST ONE DAY

To the escapee of the garden,
To thee, I sing this ode,
Wild warrior of deliverance
Who lines the side of the road.

Tawney, love-hued lily,
Do you ever pause to pray?
Just like you, well I too
Bloom for just one day.

Let's rumble the road as two,
For night won't hear our plea.
Though I picked you gently,
I believe that you picked me.

Let us bloom in auburn hues
As God rays light our way.
Hear the lesson of the lilies:
We are here for just one day.

THE COLOR OF MONSTERS

I always thought monsters were black.
They lurk in closets plotting attack,
They wear thin ties and crooked grins,
A rhyme is how their crime begins.

My best friend says they're under the bed,
Googly eyes and a bright orange head,
They see your fears whatever they be;
I'll never look, it terrifies me.

My neighbor says monsters are white,
They stalk behind you, thieving light,
They leave you blissless, lost, and blind;
I'll never watch who walks behind.

My sister says monsters are green,
The most jealous blood I've never seen.
I don't care what anyone said,
The only monsters I have met are Red.

ALBATROSS

On a night as black
    As a vulture's wing
        And cold as night wind's Sin,

We hold
We hope
We grasp
We clasp

        We will be still again.

On a night as red
As a robin's wing,

        We revel in Passion's ravine,

           We quiver
           We shiver
           We rise
           We cry

We soar like falling albatross.

           We two, we two,
           We fly.

HAIKU FOR THE ANGRY

Passionate red pulse
Quivering hands remember
Dungeoned breath escapes

RISING SUNS

After thousands of rising suns,
A bird with wings of red
Inhaled a failing breath;
His earthly hours bled.

He built a nest of spice and branch
Then faced the morning light.
He stretched his tired wings
For his final worldly flight.

A spark fell from the spirits
Onto his funeral pyre;
He sang a haunting tune,
Ascending with wings of fire.

Though seemingly alone,
Just three days had passed.
I awoke a bird rebirthed
In a pile of my father's ash.

I inhaled my opening breaths,
A phoenix with wings of red
Will see thousands of rising suns
Before my hours have bled.

Soon my breaths will cease,
I'll build my cinnamon nest
And face my final rising sun
Leaving a world I was blessed.

From my pile of feathers and ash,
Three rising suns go by;
An amber bird will emerge
Who once again will fly.

FAIRYTALE STEW

Bobbity boo
and bibbity too,
this is the story
of the fairytale stew.

With sleeping ladies
and dwarven folk too,
mice in clothing,
well, just a few.

What mixes and mingles
in this fairytale stew?
Spices with witches
and wizards too!

A cooper's hawk,
Yes it's true.
Bobbity boo
and bibbity too.

WATER HORSE

Listen, you can almost hear it
       Distant ripples of the water spirit
Emerald waters, wind, and rock
           Don't walk alone down by the loch!

Years ago, by Grandpa's pyre
       He unleashed a legend of desire
Misty, ghost-like, moonlit tide
           Resist the urge to take a ride!

Alone I stand by Loch Katrine
       I hear him breathe, but have not seen
Extended wings of the water horse
           Yet feel the wind of cold remorse

Splish, splash, waves crash; seduction takes me
       I straddle the back of the black kelpie!
Drowning, drowning, shifting power
           Folklore says it's the final hour

Listen, you can almost hear it
       Distant ripples of a stronger spirit
Emerald waters, stars, and waves
           Never lose hope for those who are brave

TWENTY-ONE

At golden Apostle sunset
Bayfield town bell tolls
A final call to pull the lines
On deck, the captain strolls.

Last remaining rays are done
A flock of gulls takes flight
They gracefully rise together
Twenty-one birds unite.

He has seen them, a time or two
They swish, they swoon, then dip
Perhaps a guise of protection
As they venture 'side his ship.

Many, many years before
The Bannockburn sank at sea
Only a flock of swirling gulls
Heard the sailors' final plea.

Twenty-one sailors salute,
Twenty-one gulls take flight,
Twenty-one angels soar the seas,
Twenty-one birds unite.

NO TRESPASSING SIGN

Snow falls upwards towards the sky
Thunder bangs through barren trees
Be prepared for raspberry rain
Sweet aroma roams the breeze.

Mountains stare at rolling fields
Where a woman lives, nobody knows
She plucks, she bends, she stoops, she tends
Her farm where chocolate grows.

Soon she'll dream, so sound asleep
In her cottage betwixt the earth
Dragonfly, mud pie, sweet lullaby
She left a cauldron upon the hearth!

No trespassing sign 'long forest lines
So I doddle there after dark
When thunder booms, I grab a spoon
A sweet voyage, I embark.

WHO KNOCKS UPON MY RUSTED DOOR?

Awakened from my
widowed dreams,
I stare upon the
cobwebbed beams.

Waves of wonder,
daybreak thunder,
I lay under
sheets of blunder.

Three knocks upon
my rusted door,
is this the one
I loved before?

Moments march
inside my head,
a vase of weeds
beside my bed.

Nightshade, barley,
creeping Charlie,
perish, perish
all I cherish.

Who knocks upon
my rusted door?
Tis just the one
I loved before.

NORTHERN LIGHTS OF NORWAY

Near the lake
I watch him pray.
In silent thought
he sits all day.

I wonder from whom
he is apart,
and feel the drumming
of his heart.

He sees me too
in reds and blues.
He hears my breath;
he's one of few.

Some days we mirror
a passing glance.
He smiles and shades
of scarlet dance.

Though many hours
he still will roam,
soon my hues will
lead him home.

Guiding, swaying
dalliance of light;
blood red, jade,
and purples ignite.

VALERIA

Valeria, Valeria
Whirling, twirling, flare
Dress of flowing sweet sangria,
Dahlia in her hair.

Dance, dance fandango
Snapping castanets
Tap, tap, tap, tap, tap, tap, stomp!
Thunderous, soulful steps.

WALTZ OF THE RED-WINGED BLACKBIRD

One, two, three
One, two, three
What have you heard?
I heard a hymn, a love song
Of a red-winged bird.

Okalee, Okalee
Who can this be?
'Tis a shadow,
Soft shadow
He's following me!

One, two, three
One, two, three
Why does he chant?
He eyes a hawk, a hunter
When my eyes can't!

MIDNIGHT AT VILLERS ABBEY

Who climbs the stairway to Villers Abbey?
Who walks this celestial place?
Candles bless, she clasps her dress
Peering through veil of lace.

Who walks the aisle of Villers Abbey?
Phantom hymn and organs sound
In barefoot bliss, she would not miss
Her vows on sacred ground.

Who awaits the altar of Villers Abbey?
Dripping candles fade to dark
Her face unveils, her skin turns pale
Not even the angels hark.

Who swarms the windows of Villers Abbey?
Who soars through broken shards?
At midnight's clock, enters a flock
Of screaming pigeons from the yard!

Who carries a message to Villers Abbey?
Who shall she love instead?
"Look inward, love, look inward."
It isn't your time for Red.

TELEPHONE BOOTH

Tumbleweed roll through desert flowers
I awake in sunrise hours
Breeze upon my waking face
Lost in a warm peculiar place.

Sky shines with ocher beams
Distant aroma of drought and dreams
Bone dry rocks adorn terrain
A land devoid of rhyme and rain.

I wipe my eyes, then compose
And trod a trail of desert rose
I hear a caw, who could that be?
A hunter perched on naked tree.

Soon he swoons then a swish
"Follow me, if you so wish."
A falcon flies the whirling wind
I follow him much like a friend.

What lies next in vast abound?
A pattering and drumming sound
Hooves are heard before they're seen
Pronghorn pass in front of me.

I feel a strange sense of dread
He stops beside my desert bed
A cowboy in a hat of straw
Smirks down on me as if in awe.

By jagged hills of snaggletooth
Stands a bright red telephone booth.
Ring, ring the rescue of a phone!
I'll leave it ring, I'm already home.

WAITING FOR RED

Who wonders what dreams befell,
In a tale too deep and dark to tell.
Once upon a moon-bathed night
Slept a woman in a cloak of white.

Wind whistled through wicked trees,
Naked branches swished with ease.
All she wished and wanted fled
O'er her malicious forest bed.

Whooshing, swooshing, slowly creeping,
Hooves approached while she lay sleeping.
She remembered him from storms ago
Before her blood was covered by snow.

A huntsman with a crooked grin
Rode miles upon miles to see her again.
He sought the one in crimson dress
With a hatchet for his love's caress.

Fairytales and flightless dreams
Fall like petals upon frozen streams.
Though she waited day and night for Red,
She chose to love herself instead.

LAST TRAIN TO BURLINGTON

What troubles
cannot be undone
on the last train
to Burlington?

Rickety rack
clickety clack,
a night train rolls
'pon icy track.

Under the glow
of blood moon light
sits a woman by name
of Scarlet Knight.

Branches tap
upon her pane,
Ms. Scarlet rides
the midnight train.

She softly wonders,
gently leaning,
tired eyes, blinks
from dreaming.

While she ponders
all she crossed,
through darkness
soars an albatross.

As he flies through
crimson light,
he is shadowed
by his flock of white.

Passing swaying
banyan trees,
branches waltz
with winter's breeze.

Why is she there?
She can't remember.
The train rolls through
a city of ember.

Smoke and fire,
screech and a scream!
The night train halts
much like a dream.

"Why, oh why
would we stop here?"
Ms. Scarlet cries
a dreadful tear.

A ring of a bell
and an, "All Aboard!"
The conductor opens
a passenger door.

A sizzling hat
and rugged boots,
in walks a cowboy
in hot pursuit!

In the dining car
she sits with he
sipping upon their
rose candy tea.

"Where were you?"
She asks Someone.
"Looking for you,
just three doors down."

"Why do you ride
the rails at night?"
asks the curious
Scarlet Knight.

So many questions,
she wasn't too late?
So many years
she had to wait!

He replies the
only thing right,
"I'm looking for
a woman in White."

"What's your name?
I have to know!"
Scarlet's hue turns
pale as snow.

With a whisper and
nod of his head,
"My name. Well,
you can call me Red."

Acknowledgements

Waiting for Red could not have been written without the patience and love of my family. Saveah, thank you for your contributions to "Fairytale Stew," "Water Horse," and "Northern Lights of Norway." Your gift of words truly inspires me. Thank you, Gavin, for your kindness and support. To my father, Carl, (June 23, 1935 – September 27, 1994), for inspiring me to live a life of passion and purpose. To my mom, Lorraine, for your gentle guidance and wisdom.

To Orange Hat Publishing, for believing in my poetry and publishing *Waiting for Red* and *In Search of the Color Yellow* as a duology. To my editor, Lauren, for your direction, detailed eye, and expertise. I am very fortunate to have collaborated with a team of professionals.

La Crosse Area Writer's Group, thank you for your friendships and loyalty to poetry. We have devoted countless hours to writing and critiquing. Thank you to the poets who share their poetry at open microphone readings, special events, and on stage at community festivals. Special thank you to those who reviewed the entire manual, as every suggestion helped to form the final story.

Thank you, Anthony, for bringing your camera into the woods for the cover photograph. Your photo perfectly captured the vision of *Waiting for Red* as a portal to a fantasy world.

Waiting for Red arrived in a daydream. Writing is weird that way, as characters enter our imaginations and refuse to leave until the last word of their story is written. Thank you, Ms. Scarlet Knight, for enticing me into your world of mirrored banyan trees and waltzing blackbirds. Finally, to the unknown cowboy, for providing hope we can all find the color Red.

K.L. Schoberg lives and writes in Southwest Wisconsin with her two children. She is a University of Wisconsin-La Crosse graduate who studied Psychology and Writing. A devoted social worker, she is committed to her community.

An advocate for poetry, Kelly organizes a monthly critique group with the La Crosse Area Writer's Group. When she is not writing, she enjoys reciting her works at open microphone events. Influences of her poetry include La Crosse Area Writer's Group, Chippewa Valley Writer's Guild, Winona Fine Arts Commission, and Wisconsin Fellowship of Poets.

Waiting for Red and *In Search of the Color Yellow* are her first published books.

klschoberg.com
Find her on Facebook: K.L. Schoberg, Author